Taking Root

A Poetic Collection

Celeste Majcher

Author: Celeste Majcher
Cover Illustrator: Elri Jacobs
First Edition 2022
Copyright © Celeste Majcher 2022
ISBN 978-1-7397164-0-0

The author can be contacted via her website:
www.celestemajcher.co.uk

To my mum, Marianna Lamprecht,
for always encouraging me to
bloom where I am planted.

I have included many blank spaces throughout this book. It is my hope that you read it with a pen and use the space to jot down your own words, ideas or images.

Motherhood

Through the Eyes of My Child

I look to the world through the eyes of
my child
I see a universe of possibilities
I see games, chances,
laughs and dances
I see a day that can be
both wonderful and wild

I look at the world with
my daughter's heart
I see suffering and hurt
I see sores to kiss better
some smiles through the years
and I pray that her compassion
will never depart

I see the world through my son's eyes
It is big, it is scary and it is uncertain
it may work, it may not,
triumph is not always a given
he may choose to never fall or fly
but oh, how I hope he would try!

For his brother this world is a battle
to conquer
a strong heart and will is mandatory.
It is a war to fight
a challenge to survive
To stay alive,
hardships simply have to be endured

And I? I see the world like my eldest does
a place of joy and suffering
in equal parts
A place to carry an immense responsibility
whilst giving thanks for the privilege
just to be

Depression

The Black Fog

The darkness of my days has been
increasing lately
And the switch to flick becomes more obscure

Do I even want to get better?
Do I need to? The answer is unsure

My family will be so much stronger
when my link can be removed
my children will know less sadness
and will only remember me as I were
a woman whole and fiery
full of life and humour
this version who I am today will be
gone forever, what a lure!

But these thoughts are distorted and untrue
and they carry only pain and illusion
'tis wise to remember that they will be gone
when this time I make it through

I am nowhere near through

I look out at the winter sun
Where does my help come from?
The cold has crept into my heart
My mind fell victim too
And though winter is ending
I still have that urge to run

I am nowhere near though

Two letters

That's all there is
between victim and victor

But in it lies a chasm so great

In the one the importance is on *me*
I am struggling
I am trying
I am unworthy
I am but human

The other highlights an alternative
a conjunction,
a pause
a possibility
or

Hope is often found in the smallest of changes
hope is often found in just two letters

Hope is the realisation that when you shift the focus
from *I am*
To the only true I AM
All will not be lost

Dark green are the walls

Dark green are the walls
that ensconce me
They feel cosy, snug
safe
warm

Lush is the velvet sofa beneath me
soft and comfy
it engulfs me
in safety

Grey is the world outside
the people are quiet
the weather is weird
the wind is tough
the world outside is cold and unforgiving
threatening and unfamiliar

I *will* venture out of my warm safety
and face the threat.
But first,
a cup of not yet

Lent

Could you do better?

Do you judge the centurion
who nailed Him to the cross,
in word and deed
and exaggerated disbelief?

Do you think you could do better?
Do you think you would?

Do you judge the king of the Jews
who saw Him as a nuisance
and sent Him on His way
not 'worth it' to be swayed?

Do you think you could do better?
Do you think you would?

Do you judge the general from Rome
who was too weak to make the right choice
too scared to use his voice
who summoned his own innocence - come!

Do you think you could do better?
Do you think you would?

How often do you walk past suffering
The hungry in the dirt
And pretend to not see them
Or to know not of their hurt?

Do you think you do better
than those so long ago?
Do you think you could?

How about that time
when you were asked to care
and knew the right thing to do
but couldn't find the will to be there?

Do you think you do better
than those so long ago?
Don't you think you should?

It's easy to feel worthy
when comparing to their sins
It's true, we have neither murdered
nor condemned;
after all, we now know better
to help Him, to defend

Surely, we wouldn't send Him to the cross?!
Surely, we wouldn't kill Him
or demand His life a loss?!

And yet, I look around with sadness
to a world more broken than before;
we may not crucify Him ourselves,
but we are worth
no more.

Crucifixion : Good Friday

Into Your Hands

He thought my fate was in his hands
He traded innocence for silver;
as reward, a life not worth living,
a life that had to end.

He thought loyalty was his to show
but, my friend,
whose life I've loved more than my own
failed me three times before the rooster's crow

His father tried to kill me once,
when I was but a babe
he mocked and ridiculed me instead
and in silence sent me to my fate

He thought me innocent and blameless
yet flogged me for their sins
he then ordered crucifixion
and washed his hands in innocence

He knew this was his story not,
the Cyrene who carried my cross
he just humbly played his part
and then left me to my lot

He thought he caused my death,
the one who drove the nails
and never would forgive himself,
not even in his dying breath

No-one really understood
and indeed, some never would.

                    God alone determines life and death

        So 'Into Your hands I commit my spirit'
        I exhaled with my final breath

Sabbath : Saturday

Nothing but Silence

What followed the day when our Saviour was lost?

The day of darkness and quakes
of spirits and shakes
when the tabernacle curtain was torn
and our doubt was born?

The voice of God Himself
told us that we should have believed
but His strength needed reprieve
and when there was none
He sighed and was gone

What followed the day when our Saviour died?
What followed was sadness
and fear and grief,
doubt, the ever-present thief
and

Silence

What followed was a deafening silence

Resurrection : Sunday

If resurrection was a colour

Palm Sunday was a joyous celebration
of hope and expectation
Its joy would tangibly have been
a luscious, deep, deep green

The Passover meal and feast
with friends gathering,
Judas' betrayal and Jesus in prison
would be no less than a bloody, brutal crimson

On Friday He died
he was beaten and crucified
The earth trembled and shook
and the silence that followed was black as soot

The Sabbath was bereft of joy and pleasure
filled with grief and longing for that which were
Life went on just as before, but those select few
sat and waited and cried,
their feelings a dark, deep blue

On day three there seemed a change in the air
it felt lighter and dare I say, bare
The tomb was empty and quiet
the women hopeful and petrified

Then Jesus appeared like the sun in the East
ever-present, ever constant, his life un-ceased
He laughed, they cried, embracing, surprised

If resurrection was a colour
it would be the glorious yellow of a new sunflower

Poems of Hope

(In 2021, I participated in a poetry challenge:
To write a poem for each day of the COP26 conference,
inspired by the focus word for each day.
This is what I came up with.)

leadership

How to lead

Look in
Earnest at
All you
Do
Does it line up with your values?
Are you true?

Love
Everyone as is
Appropriate to
Do
Do you practice what you preach?
Are you true?

Look after the
Earth, sea and skies
Attempt it at least
Discover the truths of the wise
to ensure our bad ways will cease
Do you?

There are so many options to choose from
so many paths to take
but the hardest of all,
only taken by some,
carries a responsibility you cannot shake

To lead is not simple
or easy or fun
it is daring
and tough
and caring
and rough
and not to be envied or shun'd

'Whatever you do, do it well'
is an option for some, if not all
But it is no choice, none at all,
For those who have chosen to LEAD

fragility

The most fragile of balls

the balls keep coming
and I need to keep them in the air
we are all meant to be so strong
to live this life everywhere

the balls keep coming
and I need to keep them flying
my husband, my children, my church
remain even, (un)certain and soaring

the lesser important ones get dropped
I can't keep them up any longer
and away they hop,
hop,
hop.
Ironically, it appears they're made of rubber.

School, writing, painting, the lot
they disappear from sight
until an invisible hand once again
adds them to the juggling delight

Sometimes an important one slips down
and when 'uncaught', shatters to the ground.
This week, this month, this year
the most delicate of balls is added to the mix
and I need to do my bit to also keep this
fragile, earth-shaped ball in the air

money

Five Little Coins

Hold out your hands my little dears
for inside them a pocket Pound may well appear
Now close your hands
gently, but not too tight
for these little coins can
either help you
or control you with all
their might

energy

A mother's energy

As a mother gives of herself
to her unborn child
so also gives the earth
to each a portion of her wealth

while the child dances around in her body
slowly developing, slowly maturing
the mother often loses the very essence of herself
and depletes the storehouses of her energy

the mother doesn't care, mind
for she knows it is a necessary sacrifice
to give her child its life,
a benefit in kind

But when these sacrifices keep coming
without concern for mother's health
the wealth of resources eventually dries up
and leaves the child, unable to breathe or sing

so as a child grows in a mother's womb
and matures to live a life on earth
that life needs living but can do none such
without resources of any worth

as we look after the mum to ensure
the safety of the child
we need to also look after our earth
to ensure the very breath of our lives

youth

We always wanted a voice

Children were seen and not heard when I grew up
we were ushered out to play and told not to make a fuss
and while we played, quiet, sans fuss
our world was being killed, every tree, every shrub,
and we were told it was good

because somewhere along the line
our race stopped making
and started taking
the line which was crossed was too fine
to notice from where we stood

We are no longer youths and we now see the effect
of those thoughtless years
of 'progress' and our tears
are not enough to affect
a change; but we must; we could

Today children are seen and their voices are heard
they don't take no for an answer
they stand and march where
we laughed and danced
they are making a way
and so they should

So today, we can stand and we can cry and protest
we can say we had no choice
in a time without a voice
and hope for an absolution that will never come
or with them we can stand, we can fight
without rest
                    we can fight
                                    until the fight is won

The choice we always longed for is finally ours
With it, we can clip their wings,
we still have that power,
or we can raise them up that little bit higher
and allow them their song to sing

biodiversity

The original title deed

The world was spoken into existence
and man was made
A clear distinction from the start
The world was also ours for enjoyment
but we had to play our part

we were given it to care
to grow and to plant
yet we responded with a greed that told
us to destroy, kill and steal
a greed that grew from an unfulfilled want

Now our earth's state is fatal
it's fate, at best, unsure
our plants, trees and animals
can no longer be cured
by fake promises and empty ideals

But we still have an alternative
a Hope that's real

A world that was once spoken into existence
can again be helped to exist, to thrive
if we but stop paying heed to our greed and
start taking seriously our original title deed

rest

What if we were made to rest?

What if our bodies were only made
for 6 days' work?

What if, like batteries and fitbits
and mobiles phones and laptops,
our bodies need recharging too?

What if we took a necessary break,
a weekly one,
just the one
without something pressing to do?

What if that was the plan all along?

What a strange reality that would be
at any rate.

Oh. Wait...

lament

The Earth's Lament

The earth is wailing its age-old lament:
'When will you humans ever just relent
and leave me be?
I'm tired and old and so long to be free
of your waste, your wants and your ever -
indulgent needs

I could be your best friend
your safe space to hide
a place of solace when
life no longer is on your side

Just give me a minute, a second even
to breathe
to rest, to grow, to survive
If you just give me that,
I promise not to leave

If you just give me that,
I promise those in me and on me,
that you could once again,
thrive.'

an alternate reality

An Alternate Reality

Imagine a time
when all lived in harmony
when we had all we needed
and what we had was enough.
What an alternate reality.

Imagine the time
of Adam and Eve in Eden
no reaching for forbidden fruit
no need for modesty
no break in the relationship between God
and humanity;
another alternate reality.

Now imagine a time
when people don't clamber
to get to the top
where we look out for our brother and
neighbour
and there is no such thing as human
tragedy.
What a glorious alternate reality.

movement

What moves you?

when you see a displaced child,
are you moved to tears?
when you see a redwood burn down,
do you feel your heart aching?
I see it all and feel it all
but my emotion almost never inspires action
it is too far from home,
hiding behind my just-high-enough wall

and then my child asks me why
the man outside Scotmid looks sad?
and why the children on TV are dying?
my mouth runs dry when answers evade

but his sadness moves my heart
    and my heart moves my head
        and my head moves my hands

        And with my hands
            I start a movement

build

Brick by brick he layers it

Brick by brick he layers it
with his trowel the cement gets a voice
the mixer turns and turns to prove a use
and no grain of sand is wasted, nothing
He sits and he layers all day in the heat
his back hurts, and so do his shins
but he never wonders about his cause,
not even when times are rough

Brick by brick we layer it
our little efforts of changing choice
we buy loose produce
and demand paper packaging
we walk to school and we eat less meat
and when we get a choice, we try to use our conscience
but we often wonder about our cause,
Is it enough?

The bricklayer works,
one line at a time
he builds sideways instead of upwards
and the progress is slow
We lay our efforts, one act at a time
our efforts connect and hold hands
but it is only when we stand back and look
that we notice progress inching forwards

Nothing of note gets built in a day
the number of bricks is too vast all to lay
at once or even in one go

lay them, brick by brick, they say
and at the end, when we stand back and look
we will have a healthy earth again to show

forward

Look up

We cannot go backwards
we simply cannot.
We know now the reason
and (loudly) lament our indecision
and tardy responsive reaction

Our current best efforts
are not good enough either
we cannot stand still and hope it will weather
the storms of our past
and save the lot of our future

We have to move forward
step by step, inch by metre,
It can't take forever
we simply have not that long
we need to inch forward
and attempt to do more no wrong

We know now that we should
we know now that we would
the question is therefore not one of whether,
but could?

We have to move forward,
we have to, we must
and the only way to achieve it
is to simply
look up

hope

A new hope

I was told that children are tomorrow's hope
but what chance do they have?
With no right to vote,
no voice no choice,
they are nothing but the products of our today
and with today in its current state,
tomorrow's hope stands no chance

We have to take action.
Today.
We have to give our children everything we have,
and even if that is only a fraction
of what we were given
it is still better than no hope

The world leaders of today are finally coming together
to talk, to plan, to try
we pray for wisdom,
we pray for peace,
and above all,
we pray for hope

I was told that children are tomorrow's hope
Today, we are our children's hope

Advent : Week 1

The Prophets

The wilderness shaped them
The Holy Spirit defined them
The people ignored them
Those in-the-know dismissed them
The past immortalised them
The future honoured them
The evil one could not stop them
The kings and queens could not silence them

They spoke a truth so necessary, so bare
They could not stop, they would not scare

For word of the King's first coming
was theirs
to share

Advent : Week 2

The Angel Gabriel

Does he ever tire of the light so bright with white?
Or the looks of shock and awe that inevitably follow?
Does he ever complain about the task set
or ask another messenger be sent?
Does he even have a choice?
A moment to raise his voice
of concern or doubt?
These human thoughts often fill my head
as I try to make sense of what the bible says
But the truth is I won't ever know
or in this life understand
for he is not a woman or a man
but rather a heavenly being
who in the very presence of God Himself,
may stand

Advent : Week 3

The Birth

It was a messy affair
nothing was quite right
a last-minute rush to be counted
no reservations,
no room,
no space.

But the pains had started
just as the prophecy foretold
of a king born lowly
in a stable of old
and she had no choice
but to grin and bear it.

Was she crying?
Or screaming out loud?
Or was she quietly breathing her way through it,
determined and proud?

Mary had a baby.

That is all we are told
of the labour of pain,
of the love, of the cold
of the discomfort and fear
her heart must have held
and of the exhaustion and joy
that must have dripped from her eyes in tears

Mary had a baby.

Was he dressed? Was he warm?
Did he feed well?
Or was his cry piercing and strong?

We know nothing
of those early new-born days
the birth itself is widely known
but the details will always be her own.

Mary had a baby.

Behold, the most understated sentence in all of history.

Advent : Week 4

They were wise

Of another journey we are told
in these ancient texts of note
of a caravan of travellers
with such wisdom and understanding
of stars to be bold

They travelled too far and too long
to arrive at the palace and be told that they were wrong
There had been no new baby
no royal cry
and no new heir to the throne

Yet, when they were prompted to search for and find
Him
they were wise enough to know
that their knowledge would be a threat to Him

They were wise to bring gifts
that would help Joseph escape
and provide for his family
without having to call on his name

they listened to visions in dreams and,
as foreigners
they became His first protectors

They were wise to leave when they did
and take a different route
They were wise to keep their distance
and protect His identity, they would

What a privilege to be immortalised as wise
to be known as kings with wealth to spare
but they were wise enough to know
the privilege of meeting the one true King,
was theirs.

Watchnight

The King is born

They went to sleep
between their sheep
and woke up amongst the angels

'The King is born'
they were told in chorus-song
make way, and visit him at once

for the night's not long
and before the breaking of the dawn
you need to lay your eyes upon
the new and only one, true King
Whom for all salvation brings

And finally

Sometimes

Sometimes deliverance is a deep sleep, free
from pain.
Sometimes grace looks like a happy, smiling
child.
Sometimes a mother's heart aches with the joy
and fear of release.
Sometimes a day feels like a second-long
eternity.
Sometimes deliverance looks like a tear.
And sometimes, sometimes
it is the holding of someone near.

My God, my God

My God, my God,
You have NEVER forsaken me.
When I have called out to You,
You have held me.
When I have asked for help,
You have sustained me.
When the challenges of life have felt too many,
You have carried me.
Your peace You freely give
and it is a peace I gratefully receive,
My God, my God,
You have never forsaken me.

Flourish

I see a rosebud
soft and pale and pink
It pushes through the cold snow
so crisp and fresh
proudly carrying its petals covered in the
sparkly white substance

It could have died, you know
the cold was enough to freeze the very life out of
its delicate stem
the lack of nutrition and earthy worm life could
have rendered the roots undone
and the darkness could have absorbed its natural glow

Yet,
I see a rosebud,
soft, pale and pink
pushing through the snow of hardship and
frost of challenge
rising always and rising still,
rising, as it ever will

Acknowledgements

This book would not have been possible without:

My God and King, Jesus, who made me who I am and who walks with me every step of the way.

My husband Iain, and my five greatest blessings, Andrew, Maria, Lily, Richard and William, for reminding me what life is all about.

Mr Wynand Schutte, who taught me to love poetry with some of his final breaths.

Mrs Ranza Cramer, whose English accent changed the way I read, even to this day.

Mrs Ronel Myburgh, who refused to let me speak in her class unless it was in English, and with that push, gave me the confidence I needed.